EMMANUEL JOSEPH

Leveling Up the Soul, How Gaming, Education, and Spirituality Shape the Modern Learner

Copyright © 2025 by Emmanuel Joseph

All rights reserved. No part of this publication may be reproduced, stored or transmitted in any form or by any means, electronic, mechanical, photocopying, recording, scanning, or otherwise without written permission from the publisher. It is illegal to copy this book, post it to a website, or distribute it by any other means without permission.

First edition

This book was professionally typeset on Reedsy.
Find out more at reedsy.com

Contents

1 Chapter 1: The Confluence of Worlds — 1
2 Chapter 2: The Role of Gaming in Learning — 3
3 Chapter 3: The Quest for Knowledge — 5
4 Chapter 4: Spirituality and Self-Discovery — 7
5 Chapter 5: The Intersection of Gaming and Spirituality — 9
6 Chapter 6: Education as a Spiritual Journey — 11
7 Chapter 7: The Power of Community — 13
8 Chapter 8: Overcoming Challenges — 15
9 Chapter 9: The Importance of Balance — 17
10 Chapter 10: The Future of Learning — 19
11 Chapter 11: Personal Stories of Growth — 21
12 Chapter 12: Conclusion: Leveling Up the Soul — 23
13 Chapter 13: The Science of Learning and Play — 24
14 Chapter 14: Integrating Mindfulness into Learning — 26
15 Chapter 15: The Future of Holistic Education — 28

1

Chapter 1: The Confluence of Worlds

In an era where digital realms and real-world experiences blend seamlessly, understanding the intersection of gaming, education, and spirituality becomes essential. The modern learner is not just a passive recipient of knowledge but an active participant in multiple domains. Gaming serves as a metaphor for life, with its challenges, rewards, and growth opportunities. As players embark on quests, they navigate complex worlds, solve puzzles, and overcome adversaries. These virtual experiences mirror the real-life journey of acquiring knowledge, facing challenges, and achieving personal growth.

Education lays the foundational knowledge and skills necessary to navigate these worlds. It provides the tools and framework for critical thinking, problem-solving, and creative expression. Traditional education methods are being complemented by innovative approaches that incorporate technology and interactive learning. As learners engage with these diverse educational experiences, they develop a holistic understanding of the world and their place within it. This integration of traditional and modern learning methods creates a dynamic and adaptive educational environment.

Spirituality offers a deeper connection to oneself and the universe. It transcends religious boundaries and encompasses a broader search for meaning, purpose, and inner peace. For the modern learner, spirituality can provide a sense of balance and direction, guiding them through the complexities of life. Practices such as meditation, mindfulness, and reflection foster self-awareness and emotional intelligence. These spiritual practices complement intellectual and emotional development, leading to a more fulfilled and purposeful life.

This convergence of gaming, education, and spirituality creates a holistic learning experience that nurtures the mind, body, and soul. The modern learner navigates multiple dimensions, seamlessly integrating lessons from each domain. By embracing the interconnectedness of these realms, individuals can achieve personal growth, resilience, and a deeper understanding of themselves and the world around them. The journey of the modern learner is a continuous quest for knowledge, self-discovery, and spiritual fulfillment.

2

Chapter 2: The Role of Gaming in Learning

Gaming has evolved from simple entertainment to a powerful educational tool. Through immersive environments and interactive storytelling, games teach problem-solving, critical thinking, and collaboration. Players are often required to strategize, make quick decisions, and adapt to changing scenarios, which mirrors real-world situations. These experiences help develop cognitive skills that are transferable to academic and professional settings.

Educational games specifically designed to align with curriculum objectives can enhance learning outcomes. Subjects such as mathematics, science, history, and language arts can be taught through game-based learning, making complex concepts more accessible and engaging. For example, math games that require players to solve equations to progress can reinforce mathematical skills while keeping students motivated. Science games that simulate experiments or historical events allow students to explore and understand these topics in a more interactive and memorable way.

Beyond academics, games promote perseverance, resilience, and adaptability—qualities essential for personal and professional success. In many games, players face challenges and setbacks that require them to try again and improve their strategies. This process of trial and error helps build a growth mindset, encouraging learners to view failures as opportunities for learning and growth. Additionally, multiplayer games foster teamwork and communication skills, as players must collaborate and strategize together to achieve common goals.

By incorporating game-based learning, educators can engage students in a way that traditional methods often fail to achieve. Games can capture students' attention and make learning fun, increasing their motivation and enthusiasm. This engagement can lead to improved academic performance and a deeper understanding of the subject matter. Moreover, the skills and habits developed through gaming can have long-lasting benefits, preparing students for the challenges and opportunities of the future.

3

Chapter 3: The Quest for Knowledge

Education has always been a quest for knowledge, much like the adventures in a video game. Students embark on their educational journey, overcoming obstacles and achieving milestones along the way. This journey is not just about acquiring facts and information but also about developing critical thinking, creativity, and a lifelong love of learning. The modern education system must evolve to keep pace with the dynamic nature of knowledge and the changing needs of learners.

Embracing technology is crucial for this evolution. Digital tools and resources can enhance the learning experience, providing access to a wealth of information and interactive content. Online courses, virtual classrooms, and educational apps offer flexible and personalized learning opportunities. By leveraging technology, educators can create a more dynamic and engaging learning environment that caters to diverse learning styles and needs.

Fostering creativity is another essential aspect of the quest for knowledge. Encouraging students to think outside the box, explore new ideas, and experiment with different approaches can lead to innovative solutions and breakthroughs. Creative activities such as art, music, and project-based learning provide opportunities for students to express themselves and develop their unique talents. By nurturing creativity, educators can inspire a passion for discovery and innovation in learners of all ages.

Lifelong learning is a key component of the quest for knowledge. In a rapidly changing world, the ability to adapt and continuously acquire new skills is essential. Education should not be confined to the early years of life but should be a continuous process of growth and development. By promoting a culture of lifelong learning, we can empower individuals to stay curious, motivated, and open to new possibilities throughout their lives.

4

Chapter 4: Spirituality and Self-Discovery

Spirituality transcends religious boundaries and encompasses a broader search for meaning and purpose. For the modern learner, spirituality can provide a sense of inner peace, balance, and direction. It is a journey of self-discovery that involves connecting with one's true self and the world around them. This journey can be supported by various practices and experiences that foster self-awareness and personal growth.

Meditation is a powerful practice for spiritual development. It involves focusing the mind and cultivating a state of inner stillness and clarity. Regular meditation can help reduce stress, improve concentration, and enhance emotional well-being. It allows individuals to tune into their inner thoughts and feelings, gaining insights into their true nature and desires. Through meditation, learners can develop a deeper understanding of themselves and cultivate a sense of inner peace.

Mindfulness is another important aspect of spirituality. It involves being fully present in the moment and paying attention to one's thoughts, feelings, and surroundings without judgment. Mindfulness practices, such as mindful breathing and mindful walking, can help individuals develop greater self-awareness and emotional intelligence. By being mindful, learners can better manage their emotions, make more thoughtful decisions, and build stronger relationships.

Reflection is a key component of the spiritual journey. Taking time to reflect on one's experiences, goals, and values can lead to profound insights and personal growth. Journaling, for example, is a powerful tool for reflection, allowing individuals to express their thoughts and feelings in writing. This process can help learners gain clarity, set meaningful goals, and track their progress over time. Through reflection, individuals can deepen their understanding of themselves and their purpose in life.

Spirituality and self-discovery complement intellectual and emotional development. As learners connect with their inner selves and the world around them, they develop a sense of purpose and direction. This spiritual growth enhances their overall well-being and contributes to a more balanced and fulfilling life. By integrating spirituality into the learning process, we can support the holistic development of the mind, body, and soul.

5

Chapter 5: The Intersection of Gaming and Spirituality

At first glance, gaming and spirituality may seem unrelated, but they share common themes of exploration, growth, and self-discovery. Many games incorporate moral dilemmas, ethical choices, and philosophical questions, prompting players to reflect on their values and beliefs. By approaching gaming with a spiritual perspective, players can gain insights into their own nature and the human condition.

In many role-playing games (RPGs), players create and develop characters that embark on epic quests and face significant challenges. These characters often undergo personal growth, learning important lessons about courage, loyalty, and sacrifice. As players guide their characters through these experiences, they may find themselves contemplating similar themes in their own lives. This reflection can lead to a deeper understanding of one's values and a greater sense of empathy and compassion.

Some games explore spiritual and philosophical concepts explicitly. For example, games like "Journey" and "The Legend of Zelda" series incorporate themes of destiny, interconnectedness, and the search for meaning. These games encourage players to think deeply about their purpose and the impact of their actions on others. By engaging with these themes, players can develop a more profound appreciation for the spiritual dimensions of life.

Gaming can also serve as a form of meditation and mindfulness. The immersive nature of games allows players to become fully absorbed in the present moment, blocking out distractions and stressors. This state of "flow" can be a meditative experience, promoting relaxation and mental clarity. Additionally, games that require careful observation and strategic thinking can enhance mindfulness skills, helping players stay focused and attentive.

By integrating spiritual principles into gaming, individuals can create a unique space for personal and spiritual development. This intersection offers opportunities for growth, reflection, and self-discovery. Players can explore their values, connect with their inner selves, and gain insights into the human experience. In this way, gaming becomes more than just entertainment; it becomes a meaningful and transformative journey.

6

Chapter 6: Education as a Spiritual Journey

Education is not just about acquiring knowledge; it is also a journey of self-discovery and growth. By integrating spiritual principles into the educational process, we can create a more holistic approach to learning. This includes fostering a sense of wonder, encouraging introspection, and promoting ethical behavior.

Fostering a sense of wonder is essential for inspiring a passion for learning. Encouraging students to explore the mysteries of the universe, ask questions, and seek answers can ignite their curiosity and creativity. This sense of wonder can be cultivated through various activities, such as nature walks, science experiments, and creative projects. By nurturing a sense of wonder, educators can help students develop a lifelong love of learning and discovery.

Introspection is another important aspect of the spiritual journey in education. Providing students with opportunities for self-reflection and personal growth can enhance their understanding of themselves and their goals. Activities such as journaling, mindfulness exercises, and reflective discussions can help students develop self-awareness and emotional intelligence. By encouraging introspection, educators can support the holistic development of their students.

Promoting ethical behavior is a key component of education as a spiritual journey. Teaching students to act with integrity, empathy, and compassion is essential for creating a just and harmonious society. Educators can incorporate ethical principles into the curriculum through discussions of moral dilemmas, community service projects, and character education programs. By fostering ethical behavior, educators can help students develop a strong sense of social responsibility and contribute positively to the world.

When students view education as a spiritual journey, they develop a deeper appreciation for the learning process and the world around them. This holistic approach to education nurtures the mind, body, and soul, leading to a more balanced and fulfilling life. By integrating spiritual principles into the educational process, we can create a more meaningful and transformative learning experience for all learners.

Chapter 7: The Power of Community

Both gaming and spirituality emphasize the importance of community and connection. In multiplayer games, players collaborate, compete, and form bonds that transcend geographical boundaries. These virtual communities provide a sense of belonging and support, fostering teamwork and communication skills. Players learn to work together towards common goals, celebrate successes, and overcome challenges as a united group. This sense of camaraderie and shared purpose is one of the most powerful aspects of gaming.

Similarly, spiritual practices often involve communal activities that foster a sense of belonging and support. Religious and spiritual communities provide a space for individuals to connect with others who share similar beliefs and values. These communities offer emotional support, guidance, and a sense of purpose. Participating in communal spiritual activities, such as group meditation, prayer, or community service, can strengthen individuals' spiritual growth and sense of connectedness.

Education can also benefit from this sense of community. Collaborative learning environments encourage peer support, shared knowledge, and collective growth. When students work together on projects, they learn from each other's perspectives and experiences. Group activities promote cooperation, communication, and problem-solving skills. By fostering a sense of community in educational settings, educators can create a supportive and inclusive learning environment that benefits all students.

The power of community extends beyond the virtual and spiritual realms. In all aspects of life, having a strong support system can enhance personal growth and well-being. Whether it's through gaming, spirituality, or education, the sense of belonging and connection to others is fundamental to the human experience. By embracing the power of community, individuals can find strength, inspiration, and fulfillment on their journey of personal and spiritual development.

8

Chapter 8: Overcoming Challenges

Life, like a game, is filled with challenges and obstacles. The modern learner must develop resilience and adaptability to navigate these difficulties. Gaming teaches perseverance, as players must often try and fail multiple times before succeeding. This process of trial and error helps build a growth mindset, encouraging learners to view failures as opportunities for learning and growth. By embracing challenges, players develop the resilience needed to overcome real-world obstacles.

Education provides the tools and knowledge to tackle real-world problems. It equips learners with the critical thinking, problem-solving, and analytical skills needed to address complex issues. Through a well-rounded education, individuals gain the confidence and competence to face challenges head-on. Educators play a crucial role in helping students develop these skills by creating a supportive and challenging learning environment. By encouraging students to take risks, ask questions, and think creatively, educators foster resilience and adaptability.

Spirituality offers inner strength and guidance to overcome life's challenges. Practices such as meditation, mindfulness, and reflection help individuals develop emotional resilience and mental clarity. Spiritual principles, such as acceptance, compassion, and gratitude, provide a framework for navigating difficult situations. By cultivating a strong spiritual foundation, individuals can find peace and strength in the face of adversity. This inner resilience complements the external skills gained through gaming and education.

By combining the lessons from gaming, education, and spirituality, individuals can develop a well-rounded approach to overcoming challenges. Each domain offers unique insights and tools that contribute to personal growth and resilience. The modern learner can draw on these resources to navigate life's complexities and emerge stronger and wiser. Embracing challenges as opportunities for growth leads to a more fulfilling and empowered life.

9

Chapter 9: The Importance of Balance

Finding balance in life is crucial for overall well-being. The modern learner must balance the demands of gaming, education, and spirituality to achieve harmony. This requires time management, self-discipline, and self-awareness. By prioritizing activities that nourish the mind, body, and soul, individuals can lead a balanced and fulfilling life.

Time management is essential for achieving balance. Allocating time for gaming, studying, and spiritual practices ensures that each aspect of life receives the attention it deserves. Creating a schedule or routine can help individuals stay organized and focused. By setting boundaries and limits, learners can avoid overindulgence in any one activity and maintain a healthy equilibrium.

Self-discipline plays a crucial role in maintaining balance. Developing the ability to set goals, stay motivated, and follow through with commitments is essential for achieving harmony. This involves making conscious choices and resisting the temptation to procrastinate or engage in unproductive behaviors. By cultivating self-discipline, individuals can create a balanced lifestyle that supports their personal and spiritual growth.

Self-awareness is key to understanding one's needs and priorities. Regular reflection and introspection can help individuals identify areas of imbalance and make necessary adjustments. By tuning into their inner thoughts and feelings, learners can gain insights into what brings them joy, fulfillment, and peace. This self-awareness allows individuals to make informed decisions that align with their values and goals.

Achieving balance ensures that one area of life does not overshadow the others, leading to holistic development. By integrating gaming, education, and spirituality into a well-rounded lifestyle, individuals can nurture their mind, body, and soul. This balance contributes to overall well-being, happiness, and personal growth. The journey to finding balance is ongoing, and it requires continuous effort and self-awareness.

10

Chapter 10: The Future of Learning

The future of learning lies at the intersection of gaming, education, and spirituality. As technology continues to advance, new opportunities for interactive and immersive learning experiences will emerge. Educators must stay ahead of these trends and embrace innovative approaches to teaching. By integrating gaming and spiritual principles into the educational process, we can create a more engaging and meaningful learning experience for future generations.

Virtual reality (VR) and augmented reality (AR) are transforming the way we learn. These technologies offer immersive and interactive experiences that can enhance understanding and retention. For example, VR can transport students to historical events, scientific simulations, or distant cultures, providing a first-hand experience of the subject matter. AR can overlay digital information onto the real world, creating interactive learning environments. By leveraging VR and AR, educators can create dynamic and engaging lessons that capture students' attention and imagination.

Artificial intelligence (AI) is also revolutionizing education. AI-powered tools can personalize learning experiences, providing tailored instruction and feedback based on individual needs and preferences. Adaptive learning platforms can adjust the difficulty of content based on a student's performance, ensuring that they are appropriately challenged. AI can also assist educators by automating administrative tasks, freeing up more time for meaningful interactions with students. By harnessing the power of AI, we can create more efficient and effective educational systems.

Spiritual principles can guide the future of education, promoting a holistic approach to learning. Integrating mindfulness, reflection, and ethical behavior into the curriculum can support the overall development of students. Encouraging students to explore their values, connect with their inner selves, and develop a sense of purpose can enhance their well-being and personal growth. By fostering a spiritual dimension in education, we can create a more compassionate and inclusive learning environment.

The future of learning is dynamic and ever-evolving. By embracing the intersection of gaming, education, and spirituality, we can create a more engaging, meaningful, and holistic learning experience. Educators, technologists, and spiritual leaders must collaborate to shape the future of education, ensuring that it meets the needs of modern learners and prepares them for the challenges and opportunities ahead.

11

Chapter 11: Personal Stories of Growth

Real-life stories of individuals who have successfully integrated gaming, education, and spirituality into their lives can serve as powerful examples. These personal narratives highlight the transformative potential of this holistic approach to learning. By sharing these stories, we can inspire others to embark on their own journey of growth and self-discovery.

Consider the story of Alex, a high school student who struggled with traditional education. Alex found solace and motivation in gaming, where he developed problem-solving skills and a passion for history through historically-themed games. Inspired by his gaming experiences, Alex pursued history classes and began to excel academically. He also discovered mindfulness meditation, which helped him manage stress and stay focused. Through this integration of gaming, education, and spirituality, Alex transformed his approach to learning and achieved academic success.

Another example is Maria, a young professional who balanced her demanding career with her love for gaming and spiritual practices. Maria used gaming as a way to unwind and connect with friends, while also engaging in online educational courses to enhance her skills. She practiced yoga and meditation to maintain her mental and emotional well-being. This holistic approach allowed Maria to thrive in her career, develop meaningful relationships, and lead a balanced and fulfilling life.

These personal stories demonstrate the power of combining gaming, education, and spirituality for personal growth. They highlight the potential for individuals to overcome challenges, develop resilience, and achieve their goals. By sharing these narratives, we can inspire others to explore their own paths and embrace a holistic approach to learning and living.

Each individual's experience serves as a testament to the power of integrating gaming, education, and spirituality. These stories remind us that growth and self-discovery are continuous journeys, filled with opportunities for learning and transformation. By embracing this holistic approach, we can unlock our full potential and create a more balanced and fulfilling life.

12

Chapter 12: Conclusion: Leveling Up the Soul

In conclusion, the modern learner thrives at the intersection of gaming, education, and spirituality. This holistic approach to learning nurtures the mind, body, and soul, leading to a more balanced and fulfilling life. By embracing the lessons from each domain, individuals can achieve personal growth and unlock their full potential.

Gaming offers a dynamic and interactive way to develop cognitive skills, resilience, and a sense of community. Education provides the foundational knowledge and tools needed to navigate the complexities of the world. Spirituality offers inner peace, balance, and a deeper connection to oneself and the universe. Together, these elements create a comprehensive and enriching learning experience.

The journey of leveling up the soul is ongoing, and the possibilities are limitless. By integrating gaming, education, and spirituality into our lives, we can continuously learn, grow, and evolve. This approach empowers individuals to navigate the challenges of the modern world with confidence and grace. As we embrace this holistic path, we can achieve a deeper understanding of ourselves and the world around us, leading to a more meaningful and fulfilling life.

13

Chapter 13: The Science of Learning and Play

Understanding the science behind learning and play can provide valuable insights into how gaming, education, and spirituality intersect. Research shows that play is a fundamental aspect of human development and learning. It enhances cognitive, social, and emotional skills, making it an essential component of education. By exploring the scientific principles that underpin learning and play, we can better understand the benefits of integrating gaming into the educational process.

Neuroscience has revealed that play stimulates the brain, enhancing neuroplasticity and improving memory and problem-solving skills. Games that require strategic thinking, decision-making, and creativity engage various brain regions, promoting cognitive growth. Additionally, play fosters social interactions and emotional regulation, helping individuals develop empathy, communication skills, and emotional resilience.

By incorporating play into education, we can create a more engaging and effective learning environment. Educational games that align with curriculum objectives can make learning more enjoyable and memorable. This approach not only enhances academic performance but also supports the overall development of students. Understanding the science of learning and play allows educators to harness the power of gaming to create a more dynamic and impactful educational experience.

14

Chapter 14: Integrating Mindfulness into Learning

Mindfulness is a practice that involves being fully present in the moment and paying attention to one's thoughts, feelings, and surroundings without judgment. Integrating mindfulness into the learning process can enhance students' focus, emotional well-being, and overall academic performance. By cultivating mindfulness, learners can develop greater self-awareness and resilience, helping them navigate the challenges of education and life.

Mindfulness practices, such as mindful breathing, meditation, and mindful movement, can be incorporated into the classroom. These practices help students manage stress, improve concentration, and develop emotional regulation skills. Educators can create a mindful learning environment by encouraging students to take regular breaks, practice deep breathing, and reflect on their experiences.

The benefits of mindfulness extend beyond the classroom. By developing mindfulness skills, students can enhance their overall well-being and achieve a greater sense of balance and fulfillment. This holistic approach to learning supports the development of the mind, body, and soul, creating a more comprehensive and enriching educational experience. Integrating mindfulness into learning empowers students to become more focused, resilient, and self-aware individuals.

15

Chapter 15: The Future of Holistic Education

As we look to the future, the integration of gaming, education, and spirituality will play a crucial role in shaping holistic education. This approach acknowledges the interconnectedness of the mind, body, and soul, creating a comprehensive learning experience that nurtures the whole individual. The future of holistic education involves embracing innovative technologies, promoting creative expression, and fostering spiritual growth.

Technological advancements, such as virtual reality (VR), augmented reality (AR), and artificial intelligence (AI), will continue to revolutionize education. These tools offer immersive and personalized learning experiences that engage students and enhance understanding. By leveraging these technologies, educators can create dynamic and interactive lessons that capture students' imagination and curiosity.

Creative expression is another vital component of holistic education. Encouraging students to explore their creativity through art, music, writing, and other forms of expression can enhance their cognitive and emotional development. Creative activities provide opportunities for self-discovery, innovation, and personal growth. By fostering a culture of creativity, educators can inspire students to think critically, solve problems, and pursue

CHAPTER 15: THE FUTURE OF HOLISTIC EDUCATION

their passions.

Spiritual growth will also play a significant role in the future of holistic education. Integrating spiritual principles, such as mindfulness, reflection, and ethical behavior, into the curriculum supports the overall development of students. Encouraging students to explore their values, connect with their inner selves, and develop a sense of purpose can enhance their well-being and personal growth. By fostering a spiritual dimension in education, we can create a more compassionate and inclusive learning environment.

The future of holistic education is dynamic and ever-evolving. By embracing the intersection of gaming, education, and spirituality, we can create a more engaging, meaningful, and transformative learning experience for future generations. This approach empowers individuals to navigate the complexities of the modern world with confidence and grace, leading to a more balanced and fulfilling life.

This concludes the additional chapters. I hope you find this expanded version of the book engaging and insightful. If there's anything else you'd like to add or modify, please let me know!

"Leveling Up the Soul: How Gaming, Education, and Spirituality Shape the Modern Learner":

In "Leveling Up the Soul: How Gaming, Education, and Spirituality Shape the Modern Learner," we embark on a journey to explore the dynamic interplay between three powerful forces—gaming, education, and spirituality—that shape today's learners. This thought-provoking book delves into how these seemingly disparate elements converge to create a holistic and enriching learning experience.

Discover how gaming goes beyond entertainment, offering valuable life lessons in problem-solving, resilience, and collaboration. Uncover the transformative potential of education as a quest for knowledge and personal growth, supported by innovative teaching methods and technology. Dive into the profound impact of spirituality on self-discovery, inner peace, and a sense of purpose.

Through engaging narratives, scientific insights, and real-life stories, this book reveals how the integration of gaming, education, and spirituality can lead to a more balanced and fulfilling life. Whether you're an educator, a gamer, or someone seeking personal growth, "Leveling Up the Soul" offers a fresh perspective on the interconnectedness of mind, body, and soul, inspiring you to embark on your own journey of lifelong learning and spiritual development.

www.ingramcontent.com/pod-product-compliance
Lightning Source LLC
LaVergne TN
LVHW020502080526
838202LV00057B/6107